JAMES

By their fruit you will recognize them. Do people pick grapes from thornbushes, or figs from thistles? Likewise, every good tree bears good fruit, but a bad tree bears bad fruit. A good tree cannot bear bad fruit, and a bad tree cannot bear good fruit.

– Matthew 7:16-18

Table of Contents

Introduction

Though only five chapters long, the Epistle of James has been fiercely debated by theologians because of its infamous second chapter on faith and deeds. Some theologians believed that the letter promoted a pharisaic view of justification that contradicted the message of grace espoused in other epistles, casting doubt upon its apostolic authenticity. Martin Luther called it an "epistle of straw" in an early preface to the 1522 Lutheran Bible, claiming that the letter had "nothing in it that is evangelical" when compared to the epistles of Paul, Peter, and John. Other theologians believed that the Epistle of James was integral for a holistic view on justification. John Calvin declared James as apostolic and fully inspired, arguing that it supplemented the theology of justification from Paul rather than contradict it.

Despite all this, James has been canonized into virtually every version of the Christian Bible. It has been widely quoted, memorized, preached, and taught. Its practical lessons, relatable analogies, and insightful proverbs have been a source of guidance for believers for years.

But how does the Epistle of James speak to us today? In this Bible study, we will draw closer to God through this short but powerful book.

As with every book in the Bible, learning about the author, audience, time, and place is necessary to understand its message. Familiarizing ourselves with the historical context of James will allow us to see how God's Word still speaks to us today.

Author and Audience

The author identifies himself as "James, a servant of God and of the Lord Jesus Christ" (James 1:1). Evidence suggests the author is James the Just, the brother of Jesus Christ who also appeared in the Four Gospels and the Acts of the Apostles (Matt. 13:55; Mark 6:3; John 7:5; Acts 12:7; Acts 15:13-21). James presided over the church in Jerusalem from roughly 40-62 AD. Ancient scholars theorized that James wrote his epistle in Jerusalem, a tradition that was accepted by the early church fathers Origen, Jerome, and Augustine. This view was popularized at the Council of Carthage and remained the dominant perspective until the 19th century.

Modern scholars are more divided over the author's identity. A more radical view, called the pseudepigraphic authorship view, claims that the epistle was written by a 2nd century writer who used James as a pseudonym. Another view claims that the epistle had originated from James the Just but was edited over time to be more palatable to conservative Jews.

Douglas J. Moo, author of *The Letter of James*, maintains the traditional view. James' speech in Acts 15:13-29 bears stylistic similarities to the language used by the author of James. It is commonly held that the letter was written in Jerusalem during the 1st century. These claims coincide with the years James served as overseer of the Jerusalem church.

The epistle was addressed to "the twelve tribes scattered among the nations," and its themes were especially pertinent to Jewish Christians. According to Moo, the Epistle of James refers back to more parables in the Four Gospels than any other text in the New Testament does (Moo 9). James 5:12 echoes Christ's sermon on oaths found in Matthew 5:33-37. According to Moo, this extensive knowledge of Christ's teachings demonstrates that the writer had a deep, personal relationship to Jesus Himself.

In line with Moo's analysis and the conviction of the Church Fathers, we will read the Epistle of James from the perspective that it was written by James, one of the brothers of Jesus of Nazareth (Moo 9). Moreover, we will respect the author's self-attributed title, "a servant of God and of the Lord Jesus Christ" (James 1:1), and read the book as a message that God's servant had written for us.

Since James addressed his letter to "the twelve tribes scattered among the nations" (1:1), it was most likely written for Jewish Christians in Palestine and Syria, who were descendants of the Jews who were scattered by the Assyrian Exile and Babylonian Exile. The Diaspora created a sharp disparity in wealth among the Levantine Jews. Some struggled with poverty (5:4-6; 2:6-7) while others had considerable wealth (1:10; 4:13-17).

Worldliness was a ubiquitous problem for the Jewish Christian churches. The guests whom James referred to (2:2-3) were probably rich merchants passing through the Levant. These wealthy believers were well received while the poor were treated as second-class visitors. The presence of wealth inequality, social injustices, worldliness, and changing perceptions of cultural identity are timeless themes that still resonate with modern Christians.

Genre

The Epistle of James is unique. All other epistles, particularly the Pauline epistles, adhered to Hellenic letter writing conventions. The openings named the author, the recipients, the scribe (an assistant who transcribed the author's words if the author himself was unable to write), and a courier if the letter was specially delivered. After the names, the epistles typically had a greeting – "Grace and peace to you" – followed by a prayer and word of thanks. The opening of James lacks nearly all these conventions save the author's name and intended audience.

James also tackled a wide variety of topics, swimming from one point to the next. In contrast, each of the respective Pauline epistles focuses on a central theme and follows a tight narrative framework. Because of this, James has been categorized as wisdom literature, a Biblical genre that includes books such as Proverbs, Job, Psalms, and Ecclesiastes. James has been informally referred to as the Christian Proverbs, providing moral instruction through a copious citation of traditional precepts and observations made from eclectic sources. Modern scholars, however, have argued that reading James as wisdom literature may be inaccurate since James does focus on a few central themes that hold the book together. Instead, they have proposed that James is more like an ancient sermon that a pastor preaches to his beloved church members, focusing on the most pressing matters that are affecting the church.

Theology

The first theme that James raises is suffering (1:2-4; 1:12-15), a state that characterized much of Jewish history. The Babylonian Exile and Assyrian Exile uprooted the Jews from their ancestral home and spread them across the Levant. They were forced to leave Jerusalem and abandon the Holy Temple in Jerusalem, their central place of worship. The Jews of James' time were descended from those captives, fractured into various sects that all lived under the hegemony of the Roman Empire. They wondered how God could allow them to suffer such terrible events.

James believed that suffering was not direct persecution but instead a test (πειρασμος, *peirasmos*). According to James, Job demonstrated the proper reaction to suffering by refusing to curse God and enduring in patience. Through this, Job was rewarded with greater perseverance and maturity. However, Christians are promised more than just character for overcoming hardship. As theologian Peter Davids writes, "The need of the moment is not resistance to evil, but perseverance in the good. The church needs to hold together in the face of the intense pressure upon it while it, like Job, awaits the resolution of the eschatological battle" (Davids 38).

For James the Just, all of suffering was a precursor to Christ's return. He organized his actions and beliefs around this expectancy:

> Be patient, then, brothers and sisters, until the Lord's coming. See how the farmer waits for the land to yield its valuable crop, patiently waiting for the autumn and spring rains. You too, be patient and stand firm, because the Lord's coming is near. Don't grumble against one another, brothers and sisters, or you will be judged. The Judge is standing at the door! (James 5:7-9)

The Lord will return to judge, and that judgment will be based upon a believer's spiritual harvest. Because of this, James urged Christians against seeking out wealth like the people of the world (1:9; 5:1-6). Instead, he reminded them of their mortality and implored them to follow the will of God (4:14-15). By drawing near to God and dwelling with Him, the believer can be freed from the world's temptations (4:1-8). Intimacy with God begins through salvation (1:18) and repentance (4:6) but is manifested and verified through virtuous deeds.

A Christian who receives the Gospel, that Jesus Christ saved us through His crucifixion and resurrection as planned by the Father and testified to us by the Holy Spirit, cannot remain inert. Faith that does not produce action is dead (2:17). Actions do not earn salvation, but they do demonstrate that a believer's faith is strong and alive (Matt. 7:17). James instructed his audience on how to put the Word of God into action through the particular importance of charity and giving (James 1:19-27).

References

Davids, Peter H. The Epistle of James: A Commentary on the Greek Text. Grand Rapids, MI: Eerdmans, 1982. Print.

The Holy Bible: New International Version. Grand Rapids, MI: Zondervan, 2005. Print.

Moo, Douglas J. James (Tyndale New Testament Commentaries). Grand Rapids, MI: IVP Academic, 2009. Print.

How to Read This Book

"Anyone who listens to the word but does not do what it says is like someone who looks at his face in a mirror and, after looking at himself, goes away and immediately forgets what he looks like. But whoever looks intently into the perfect law that gives freedom, and continues in it – not forgetting what they have heard, but doing it – they will be blessed in what they do."
James 1:23-25

The Word of God is in one sense a mirror. By looking into it, we see what God wants us to become: the perfect image and love of Christ. But our hearts are quick to forget what God is trying to show us. If we consider the Word of God with only furtive glances, James says we will become strangers to the face of Jesus. The purpose of this book is to turn those glances into an intent gaze that is aimed directly at our Savior so that His perfect law will continue to free and transform us throughout our mornings, our nights, and our Sunday services.

This James book is a month-long, inter-ministry Bible study on the Epistle of James, split into three elements we like to call **praying**, **professing**, and **preaching**.

Praying: Daily Devotionals

The devotionals contextualize the Epistle of James by providing illustrations, reflection questions, and prayer topics each day. Read them in a quiet part of your home or office. Don't rush through them. Give them time to soak in your heart. Most importantly, pray. Reflect upon the passage throughout your day. These devotionals are designed to supplement your personal prayer and meditation, not replace them.

Professing: Corporate Bible Studies

The Bible studies can be used by any group that meets weekly. They highlight key verses and expand upon the illustrations of the daily devotionals. Each study ends with a reflection question for group discussion. Don't be shy! Profess your insights! God will use you to encourage and challenge your brothers and sisters.

Preaching: Sunday Sermons

The Sunday sermons are inspired from the same passages and key verses found in the devotionals and Bible studies. They are the culmination of a week's worth of prayer, meditation, and group discussion, bringing the reader into a greater understanding of God through the Epistle of James. Carry each Sunday message with you beyond the church walls by utilizing the ten pages of space allotted for ample note-taking.

This book is best used in a church or a group ministry setting. Each program in the book is meant to build up the Body of Christ: the individual grows through devotionals, small groups grow through the Bible studies, and the whole body is built up when everyone comes together for the sermon. Through the daily devotionals, weekly Bible studies, and Sunday sermons, we pray that God's Word will make an indelible mark on your heart.

May you never forget the reflection of our Lord's beautiful face presented to us in the Epistle of James.

Daily
Devotionals

Introduction

In this section, the five chapters of the Book of James are divided into 24 devotionals for a more concentrated reading each day.

Begin with reading the Bible passage to yourself once, twice, or perhaps even more times, and then, read the devotional that follows. Reflect upon both throughout the day and pen your thoughts into writing on the blank spaces provided. Each devotional closes with a prayer line to help begin your own prayer at the end. See how your reflection grows and heart is convicted as you pray that prayer line throughout the day.

Keep in mind that, while these devotionals break up the epistle into smaller-sized consumption for daily intake, they aren't discrete, unrelated passages that speak into just one sin, struggle, or theme at a time. Rather they work together to speak an overall message on faith. See how the devotionals progress and engage with one another to challenge your walk not only today but for every day.

As you beseech the Lord in these next four weeks through the teachings of James, may the Word of God truly illuminate every crevice and corner of your heart to a greater worship of Him.

Day 1

"James, a servant of God and of the Lord Jesus Christ, to the twelve tribes scattered among the nations: Greetings. Consider it pure joy, my brothers and sisters, whenever you face trials of many kinds, because you know that the testing of your faith produces perseverance. Let perseverance finish its work so that you may be mature and complete, not lacking anything."
James 1:2-4

In his letter to the early Christians, the first topic James wrote about was suffering. He raised the age-old question we still ask today: Why does God allow the righteous to suffer? This is indeed a perplexing question for all believers. It must have been an extremely painful one for the persecuted Christians who received this letter. Yet James writes that they should consider their sufferings "pure joy." Why?

What could be the benefit of living through hardships? According to James 1:3-4, the benefit is that our faith can grow in discipline and perseverance. We need discipline for perseverance, to keep going, keep trusting, and keep believing even when our circumstances, our friends, and our own bodies give up on us through suffering. When 1:4 says that we will become "mature and complete, not lacking anything," it means that our faith will become so disciplined that we will be equipped and useful for God's kingdom work in any situation.

If a chef wants to prepare high-quality soup, he must boil his ingredients overnight or even for several days to produce a rich, hearty stock. Can you imagine a bowl of pho or Korean ox-tail soup with thin, watery broth? The stock is the foundation of the soup. If the stock is bad, no amount of extravagant garnish will improve the taste!

Remember Jesus' words in Matthew 5:13 when He stated that we are the "salt of the earth":

> You are the salt of the earth. But if the salt loses its saltiness, how can it be made salty again? It is no longer good for anything, except to be thrown out and trampled underfoot.

Our lives are useless when they are tasteless. We become saltier when we are boiled for an extended time, suffering and learning to discipline our faith. Like soup that is being reduced, God prunes out our idols like water while thickening and intensifying our flavor.

The result is a Christian who will not be shaken by circumstances, people, or the temptations of this world. This is why our sufferings are "pure joy": because God is fulfilling Matthew 5:13 in us when we endure suffering.

It is through hardship that we become the salt of the earth, disciplined and tasty for God and for others to enjoy!

Reflection

Write down the biggest trial in your life at this time. List the ways you have been responding to them. After reading James 1:2-4, write down how you want to respond to them as a test of your faith to build perseverance.

Dear Lord, it is my upmost joy to serve You. Give me the strength to endure my battles, fortify me with the armor of God. I will not stand down to the enemy. May perseverance finish its work in my life!

Day 2

*"If any of you lacks wisdom, you should ask God, who gives
generously to all without finding fault, and it will be given
to you. But when you ask, you must believe and not doubt,
because the one who doubts is like a wave of the sea, blown
and tossed by the wind. That person should not expect to
receive anything from the Lord. Such a person is double-
minded and unstable in all they do."*
James 1:5-8

In 2011, Google released the ten most popular inquiries
on its search engine:

1. What is Love?
2. What is Planking?
3. What is Twitter?
4. What is Gluten?
5. What is Skype?
6. What is Dubstep?
7. What is Autism?
8. What is Lupus?
9. What is Gout?
10. What is Google+?

The popularity of the number one question didn't surprise
me at all, but I was quite concerned that so many were asking one of life's most important and philosophical questions through Google.

If we want to use a MacBook to the fullest, it would
be common sense to take it to an Apple store. If we want
to best utilize a ThinkPad, we would consult its creator,
IBM. Likewise, if we want to live our lives to the fullest, we must find the One who created mankind. If we
want to live in this world properly, we need to seek the

One who created the world! In John 10:10, Jesus said that "the thief comes only to steal and kill and destroy; I have come that they may have life, and have it to the full." He promises us a full life!

Our devotional verse for today highlights this idea. If you want to live a better life, come to the One who created you for answers and wisdom! Learn how to navigate the world from its Creator!

Reflection

Where have you looked for wisdom outside of God? What kind of wisdom did you gain from these other sources? How might God's wisdom compare to the wisdom you gained from this world?

Father God, I ask of You this day to give me my daily bread. Grant me a sound mind in any and every situation. Your wisdom is the wellspring of my life. Show me Your ways, for they are better than gold, sweeter than honey. Speak, O Lord, for I am listening.

Day 3

"Believers in humble circumstances ought to take pride in their high position. But the rich should take pride in their humiliation – since they will pass away like a wild flower. For the sun rises with scorching heat and withers the plant; its blossom falls and its beauty is destroyed. In the same way, the rich will fade away even while they go about their business."
James 1:9-11

In these verses, James discusses the power of money, an idol with which we all wrestle. Our text today shows that money is a struggle not only for the rich but also the poor. Notice how James addresses all of the Jews of the twelve tribes as "brothers" in James 1:2, regardless of wealth or financial standing. Being rich or poor isn't the issue at hand.

The real issue is this: Does your wealth or poverty taint God's view of who you are? If you feel as though God's view of you is determined by how much or how little you have, then, you are failing the test.

If you are indeed poor, you may believe what the world says about you. You will feel powerless and insecure. Yet James reminds the poor that they are co-heirs, sons and daughters of King Jesus who have been lifted up to the highest of all creation. They should be meditating on their identity and relationship with Jesus Christ.

Likewise, for the rich, James reminds you that all of your riches will wither away like grass. What are your possessions compared to the treasures of Jesus? Withering grass. As you scurry about in your business, remember that everything you make and have will vanish as quickly as weeds die. Therefore, do not waste time on loving money but instead love Christ. This is the sobering reminder that James leaves to all of us, rich and poor.

Reflection

In Matthew 6:24, Jesus said:

> No one can serve two masters. Either you will hate the one and love the other, or you will be devoted to the one and despise the other. You cannot serve both God and money.

Are you serving God or money today? Where do you devote your time, energy, talents, and heart?

You are the Lord of my life; I surrender my finances, my time, my talents, and my heart. If there is anything else that I have yet to surrender, please show me, dear Lord, and I will be quick to relinquish all of it to You. Here I am, take it all! I hold nothing back.

Day 4

*"Blessed is the one who perseveres under trial because,
having stood the test, that person will receive the crown
of life that the Lord has promised to those who love him.
When tempted, no one should say, 'God is tempting me.'
For God cannot be tempted by evil, nor does he tempt
anyone; but each person is tempted when they are dragged
away by their own evil desire and enticed. Then, after
desire has conceived, it gives birth to sin; and sin, when it is
full-grown, gives birth to death. Don't be deceived, my dear
brothers and sisters. Every good and perfect gift is from
above, coming down from the Father of the heavenly lights,
who does not change like shifting shadows. He chose to give
us birth through the word of truth, that we might be a kind
of firstfruits of all he created."*
James 1:12-18

Sadly, the trials mentioned in James 1:12 of today's passage happen all too often in our lives. As a pastor, I counsel many people who go through hard times like poverty, job loss, broken relationships, sickness, and the death of loved ones. These trials lead many people to temptation, putting them at risk to major sins, such as doubt, anger, and unbelief. They become like the man in this passage who blames God and says, "God is tempting me."

Though it may feel natural for us to attribute our trials to others, James warns us not to cast blame upon anyone – not God and not even the Devil.

The Scottish poet Robert Burns once wrote:

> Thou knowest that Thou hast formed me.
> With passions wild and strong,
> And, listening to their witching voice,
> Has often led me wrong.

Like Adam and all his descendants, Robert Burns blames God for our wild instincts, but James instructs us to look inward.

While it is true that God allows trials and tests, He does not permit these things so that we may be tempted. He seeks to develop our moral qualities and build our character. Through my own trials, God has dug through the innermost chambers of my heart and exposed idols I would have never discovered on my own. God brings these things to the forefront so we may cling to Him more, leading us to the ultimate good which is Himself!

What about you? How do you deal with failures and unsuccessful ventures? Do you feel snubbed? Do you feel like a victim? Bitter, lonely, or hurt?

We must think deeply and honestly to see the spiritual bankruptcy within us. Did you really leave your job because of your boss? Did you really leave church because of your cell group? What "evil desires" were in your heart?

Reflection
James warns us that our evil desires can give birth to sin. Ask the Lord to help identify any evil desires in your heart and take time to repent before God.

Will You give me eyes to my own heart? May the sins that plague my heart be burned in the fire, for I only want to live for one thing: the crown of life that You promise to those who love You.

Day 5

*"My dear brothers and sisters, take note of this: Everyone
should be quick to listen, slow to speak and slow to become
angry, because human anger does not produce the righteousness that God desires. Therefore, get rid of all moral
filth and the evil that is so prevalent and humbly accept the
word planted in you, which can save you. Do not merely
listen to the word, and so deceive yourselves. Do what it
says. Anyone who listens to the word but does not do what
it says is like someone who looks at his face in a mirror
and, after looking at himself, goes away and immediately
forgets what he looks like. But whoever looks intently into
the perfect law that gives freedom, and continues in it – not
forgetting what they have heard, but doing it – they will be
blessed in what they do."*
James 1:19-25

At first glance, what James shares here seems like conventional wisdom. Secular counselors would agree that we
ought to listen more and be slower to speak. However, we
must keep in mind that Scripture always goes deeper than
face value.

In the previous verses (James 1:1-19), James speaks
about the importance of perseverance, listing all of its
benefits and encouraging struggling Christians with
words of wisdom so that they may persevere through the
trials and suffering, whether the suffering was poverty or
materialism (1:9-11) or the consequences of sin (1:12-15).
In this context, James was speaking directly to people who
were suffering. When they suffered, how did they respond
with their words? Perhaps they spoke rashly in anger and
slander. We can recognize when someone is suffering by
the words that come out of his or her mouth.

"Don't you see that whatever enters the mouth

goes into the stomach and then out of the body? But the things that come out of a person's mouth come from the heart, and these defile them. For out of the heart come evil thoughts – murder, adultery, sexual immorality, theft, false testimony, slander. These are what defile a person; but eating with unwashed hands does not defile them" (Matt. 15:17-20).

Bitter and angry words are the symptoms of a weary heart. When we are going through difficult times, it's natural and easy for us to call people and vent. We are short-fused during these times and can snap when we can't handle things anymore. We make mistakes more easily and can even sever our relationships, only to regret our decisions later when the trial is over and we're thinking clearly once more.

Therefore, when we go through trials, we need to remember that these times are given from the Lord for a specific purpose, and we must be slow to speak and quick to listen intently.

In his book, *The Problem of Pain*, C.S. Lewis writes, "Pain insists upon being attended to. God whispers to us in our pleasures, speaks in our consciences, but shouts in our pains. It is his megaphone to rouse a deaf world."

Reflection

Are your words edifying or condemning? Do you see yourself venting and speaking ill of people? Let's examine our hearts this morning and see if you have responded correctly to the difficult challenges in your life. Listen to those around you. Turn your ear to the gentle voice of our Father who loves and cares for you.

Father God, will You give me listening ears and an open mind? Help my heart to be teachable, may Your word transform me day in and day out. I refuse to allow my mouth to condemn and to judge others any longer. May my lips be a fountain of worship and nothing less.

Day 6

"Those who consider themselves religious and yet do not keep a tight rein on their tongues deceive themselves, and their religion is worthless. Religion that God our Father accepts as pure and faultless is this: to look after orphans and widows in their distress and to keep oneself from being polluted by the world."
James 1:26-27

Most of you readers are "religious people" in the eyes of the world. Earlier in the chapter, James said that the Word of God transforms our lives and gives us a new birth. Furthermore, he emphasized that this new birth must be followed not only by hearing the Word of God but also by persistence and obedience. In these verses, James explains true religion.

Without understanding the purpose of good works, we can fall into the trap of believing that good works constitute a true religion, but false religions emphasize good works, too. Our understanding of God's love should certainly lead us to good works, but true religion is discovered when we examine why we do good works. Some people feel religious when they see suffering and are convicted to donate some money, falling into a sporadic habit of "do good-ism." Others can gain a false sense of piety by donating a large sum of money and never missing a Sunday service or quiet time.

However, by mentioning bridling of the tongue (James 1:26), James reveals that strengthening our inner being takes priority over our good acts. In Ephesians 3:16, Apostle Paul makes a similar comment:

> I pray that out of his glorious riches he
> may strengthen you with power through

his Spirit in your inner being.

Earlier in the chapter, James explained that what comes out of our mouths is an internal matter. What resides in our hearts and thoughts surface through our public and private conversations, Facebook updates, and diaries.

We can easily do good works to selfishly praise ourself and feel good about our contributions. Therefore, James wants our heart's motivation checked behind every good deed. Furthermore, he specifically mentions caring for widows and orphans. Can widows and orphans, who were the most marginalized individuals during James' time, be properly cared for through spontaneous visits and gifts? Notice that "Look after" is written in the present tense. James stresses that true care is habitual and persistent.

Reflection

Ask yourselves, Am I an obedient doer of God's Word? What are my heart's motives when I do something good? Are my deeds faithful and persistent or circumstantial according to what is convenient for me?

You are a God who looks at my heart. My boasting and great feats are meaningless without my heart. Strengthen my inner man, O Lord! I want to live a life pursuing after one thing: Your glorious name and Your renown.

*"My brothers and sisters, believers in our glorious Lord Je-
sus Christ must not show favoritism. Suppose a man comes
into your meeting wearing a gold ring and fine clothes, and
a poor man in filthy old clothes also comes in. If you show
special attention to the man wearing fine clothes and say,
'Here's a good seat for you,' but say to the poor man, 'You
stand there' or 'Sit on the floor by my feet,' have you not
discriminated among yourselves and become judges with
evil thoughts? Listen, my dear brothers and sisters: Has not
God chosen those who are poor in the eyes of the world to
be rich in faith and to inherit the kingdom he promised
those who love him? But you have dishonored the poor. Is it
not the rich who are exploiting you? Are they not the ones
who are dragging you into court? Are they not the ones
who are blaspheming the noble name of him to whom you
belong?"*
James 2:1-7

In Chapter 2, James expands upon the theme of hearing the
word and obeying it (James 1:22) by addressing favoritism
in the early church. In this text, the English word "favoritism" is translated from the Greek word προσωπολημψίαις
(*prosōpolēmpsiais*), referring to any sort of partiality or
prejudice.

Do you think the Indian caste system is a good idea?
What about the American slave trade? If anybody were
to voice support for these institutions on Facebook, what
would the consequences be in our society? I know one
thing for sure – I wouldn't want to be that person!

Most people in our society would condemn the caste
system of India and the Transatlantic Slave Trade as if we
would never support those things even if we were Indian
or white males in Colonial America. According to James,

however, we are no different from slavers or bigots when we show partiality towards people because of their possessions, looks, gender, or race. Because of our sinful bias, there is an invisible caste system in America, too. How many times have we seen investigative news reports and hidden camera shows that revealed our preference for good-looking and rich people, from getting jobs to receiving favors on the street? Are we really any different from our ancestors?

James stresses two big reasons for why we should not show favoritism. First, it is because we should not disgrace "our glorious Lord Jesus Christ" (2:1) by showing favoritism, especially to the rich. His love is unconditional and perfect for all. By holding prejudice against others, particularly against the poor, we dishonor God Himself. Secondly, in Matthew 6:24, Jesus said, "No one can serve two masters. Either you will hate the one and love the other, or you will be devoted to the one and despise the other. You cannot serve both God and money." When we show favoritism to the rich, it indirectly reveals our true master.

Remember today that your favoritism of people unearths the idols of your heart and reveals your true master!

Reflection

Think about the people you interact with on a daily basis at home, at work, or at church. How have you shown favoritism? What does your favoritism reveal about your own heart and what you desire?

Father God, show me the idols that I secretly covet in my heart. Forgive me, my Lord, for I have pursued a life of wealth and recognition in the world. I have judged men by my own standards. I declare that my wealth is in You alone! You are my portion and my prize, my crown jewel.

Day 8

"If you really keep the royal law found in Scripture, 'Love your neighbor as yourself,' you are doing right. But if you show favoritism, you sin and are convicted by the law as lawbreakers. For whoever keeps the whole law and yet stumbles at just one point is guilty of breaking all of it. For he who said, 'You shall not commit adultery,' also said, 'You shall not murder.' If you do not commit adultery but do commit murder, you have become a lawbreaker. Speak and act as those who are going to be judged by the law that gives freedom, because judgment without mercy will be shown to anyone who has not been merciful. Mercy triumphs over judgment."
James 2:8-13

In this portion of the text, James continues on the topic of favoritism. If James 2:1-7 were a warning against favoritism, then, 2:8-13 is an in-depth teaching of why it's a big sin.

While he was studying in South Africa, Mahatma Gandhi spoke about a time when he read the Gospels seriously and considered converting to Christianity. He believed that he could find the solution to the caste system, which was dividing the people of India, in the teachings of Jesus, so one Sunday he decided to attend services at a nearby church and talk to the minister about becoming a Christian. When he entered the sanctuary of a Caucasian church, the usher refused to give him a seat and suggested that he go worship with his own people. Gandhi left the church and never returned. "If Christians have caste differences also," he said, "I might as well remain a Hindu."

As we see from this testimony of Gandhi, that church he visited was guilty of breaking the royal law of "Love your neighbor as yourself." James here stresses not only that as Christians unfair partiality betrays Jesus but also that it hinders the gospel work (2:12-13). We turn people away from trusting Jesus as Savior.

In the Lord's Prayer, Jesus taught us to ask God to "forgive us our as we also have forgiven our debtors." In 1 Corinthians 13:1, Paul echoes this call for mercy by saying, "If I speak in the tongues of men or of angels, but do not have love, I am only a resounding gong or a clanging cymbal." James also expounds on this concept with his own words in James 2:13.

Showing mercy to the weak has redeeming qualities. If we can't show mercy to the weak, how can we expect to escape God's judgment? Our forgiveness and acceptance of others prolong and strengthen God's forgiveness over our lives!

Mercy triumphs over judgment!

Reflection

Meditate on your interactions with people from the past week. Have you been judging anyone for past or present faults or annoyances? How does God want you to show mercy?

Teach me, O Lord, what it means to truly love my neighbor as myself. Show me the way of mercy. May it be more than just my words or my deeds, but Your compassion filling my heart to give, to love, and to serve today.

Day 9

*"What good is it, my brothers and sisters, if someone
claims to have faith but has no deeds? Can such faith save
them? Suppose a brother or a sister is without clothes and
daily food. If one of you says to them, 'Go in peace; keep
warm and well fed,' but does nothing about their physical needs, what good is it? In the same way, faith by itself,
if it is not accompanied by action, is dead. But someone
will say, 'You have faith; I have deeds.' Show me your faith
without deeds, and I will show you my faith by my deeds.
You believe that there is one God. Good! Even the demons
believe that – and shudder."*
James 2:14-19

Our text today has inspired many discussions and con-
troversies in the church. Some Christians believed these
verses disproved the doctrine of *sole fida*, or salvation by
faith alone. Some have even doubted their salvation after looking at their lives to find a lack of good deeds and
transformations. I would like to address these concerns
by sharing the wisdom I have gained from meditating on
these texts over the years. I hope it will guide many of us
towards a better understanding of our faith.

The "dead faith" that James had in mind is similar to
what John the Baptist spoke about at the Jordan River in
Matthew 3:5-10:

> People went out to him from Jerusalem
> and all Judea and the whole region of the
> Jordan. Confessing their sins, they were
> baptized by him in the Jordan River. But
> when he saw many of the Pharisees and
> Sadducees coming to where he was baptiz-
> ing, he said to them: "You brood of vipers!

> Who warned you to flee from the com-
> ing wrath? Produce fruit in keeping with
> repentance. And do not think you can say
> to yourselves, 'We have Abraham as our
> father.' I tell you that out of these stones
> God can raise up children for Abraham.
> The ax is already at the root of the trees,
> and every tree that does not produce
> good fruit will be cut down and thrown
> into the fire."

By referencing today's text with this passage, we see that
James and John were condemning the Sadducees and the
Pharisees who overemphasizied works and legalism as the
way to salvation. But why did John rebuke them when
they came to receive baptism? Because they believed baptism and good deeds were contributing to their salvation.
Their goal was to earn spiritual brownie points through
baptism without genuine repentance. They weren't concerned about God; they were concerned about themselves.

Repenting is realizing that nothing we do can earn
salvation, because our deeds will never be good enough
for our perfect God. Instead we despair and mourn before
God, knowing that we are totally depraved and hopeless
and can only trust in His grace shown upon the cross for
salvation.

According to James, those who have tasted the unilateral grace of God and are saved by His perfect love on the
cross will inevitably be moved to do good works. However, our motivation for good deeds is vastly different than
that of the Sadducees and the Pharisees. John the Baptist
described their deeds as fruit that does not keep with repentance. Their deeds were essentially rotten fruit. People who are loved by God do not earn saving points with
good deeds. We are already saved by the blood of Christ!

Rather we do good deeds out of our love for God. This is the mark of a tree bearing good fruit.

Reflection

Paul told the Philippians to "work out your own salvation with fear and trembling, for it is God who works in you both to will and to do for His good pleasure" (Phil. 2:12-13). God unilaterally saved us, and He works in us so that we may learn to obey Him. At the same time, God asks us to work out our salvation, meaning that we need to personally experience God's work in our lives and act upon God's presence in our lives. Here is a helpful list of things to remember as you work out your salvation:

1. **W**alk at your own pace! Work out your salvation to the best of your ability. Always challenge the limits of your spiritual endurance, but don't think your faith is not genuine just because your testimony is different from a popular pastor's!

2. **O**vercome sin through endurance! When we fall to sin, the Enemy magnifies that failure so that we become disillusioned by guilt, blinding us from seeing the spiritual progress we've made. Satan is the one behind all the guilt trips. God leads us to redemption through conviction, not condemnation.

3. **R**emember your former hopeless state and the great love that delivered you! Recalling the grace and love of the cross will activate your faith (John 3:16) and sustain you during times of spiritual depression.

4. **K**neel before the cross and acknowledge its complete redemptive power! You have been reborn through the unilateral grace on the cross, but your spiritual growth is bilateral. Do everything in your power to capitalize upon God's redeeming grace.

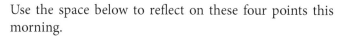

Use the space below to reflect on these four points this morning.

Father God, will You show me how to live out my faith with my hands and my feet? To love because You love, to serve because You served? Oh, to be a fruitful tree planted by Your streams of living water!

Day 10

> *"You foolish person, do you want evidence that faith without deeds is useless? Was not our father Abraham considered righteous for what he did when he offered his son Isaac on the altar? You see that his faith and his actions were working together, and his faith was made complete by what he did. And the scripture was fulfilled that says,*
> *"Abraham believed God, and it was credited to him as righteousness," and he was called God's friend. You see that a person is considered righteous by what they do and not by faith alone. In the same way, was not even Rahab the prostitute considered righteous for what she did when she gave lodging to the spies and sent them off in a different direction? As the body without the spirit is dead, so faith without deeds is dead."*
> *James 2:20-26*

In the previous passages, James demonstrated two kinds of faith that are insufficient. The first was the "dead" faith (James 2:17) of the Pharisees and Sadducees in Matthew 3:7 – belief without any action. The second was the faith that even demons have (James 2:19), rebelling against the Word of God despite accepting its truth.

In today's text, he discusses "useless" faith (4:20). Useless faith has no tangible evidence. It's all words and no power, as Paul describes in 1 Corinthians 13:1:

> If I speak in the tongues of men or of angels, but do not have love, I am only a resounding gong or a clanging cymbal.

Thankfully, James concludes his lesson by showing us an example of genuine faith. Genuine faith originates in grace and the love of God but is verified through loving

God through loving others. In other words, good deeds!

In fact, Abraham, too, was tested in faith and verified by deeds. Genesis 15:6 says, "Abram believed the LORD, and he credited it to him as righteousness." Abraham was credited as righteous only because of his trust in God! However, once he believed and the righteousness of God was imputed to him, his faith was tried in Genesis 22 and ultimately attested through his selfless obedience to God.

Paul, who preached "justification by faith," and James, who preached "justification by faith and works," were actually in agreement. Paul was simply emphasizing spiritual birth while James emphasized spiritual growth. With that in mind, the argument in the text becomes quite simple and obvious. If God unilaterally saved our spirit and conscience through the death and resurrection of Jesus Christ, then, God's righteousness is now our new identity and His Holy Spirit lives within us. Wouldn't you then say that it's impossible for this person to remain the same?

If there are people who completely change their lifestyle after a near death experience or emergency rescue, how can we remain the same after God has rescued our eternal souls – the very climax and culmination of all of redemptive history? This is James' argument! Show me your faith!

Reflection

Consider how you practice your faith on a daily basis. What is one daily habit that you can adopt or change to put your faith into action? Is there something you can do to demonstrate God's mercy to your family members? Co-workers and colleagues? Friends? The poor and needy?

You have loved me with an everlasting love. It is simply impossible for me to ever be the same again! How may I show You that my love for You is real? Show me what to say and what to do so that my life may bear testimony of Your sacrifice on the cross for someone like me.

Day 11

*"Not many of you should become teachers, my fellow be-
lievers, because you know that we who teach will be judged
more strictly. We all stumble in many ways. Anyone who is
never at fault in what they say is perfect, able to keep their
whole body in check. When we put bits into the mouths
of horses to make them obey us, we can turn the whole
animal. Or take ships as an example. Although they are so
large and are driven by strong winds, they are steered by a
very small rudder wherever the pilot wants to go. Likewise,
the tongue is a small part of the body, but it makes great
boasts. Consider what a great forest is set on fire by a small
spark."*
James 3:1-5

On the surface, James' opening warning seems harsh:
Don't desire to teach, because you will be judged more
strictly! However, in the audience James addressed, there
were most likely some who desired to be teachers but were
not yet qualified to teach. In James 3:2, he empathetically
notes that "we all stumble in many ways," which we can
all attest to quite readily without pause. Yet in 3:2b, James
gives us an understanding of what a perfect man is. A perfect man does not stumble with his words, and as a result,
his *whole* body is also kept in line.

What a man has to say overlaps *wholly* with *how he
lives*, and James continues this theme with the analogies
he provides in 3:3-4. There is a connection between what
a man says and the holistic conduct of his life. James describes how we can be thoroughly righteous. When our
talk and our conduct align perfectly, they cannot contradict each other.

Having understood James' point, our rereading of
3:1 should become clearer. We should not desire to be

teachers, because teachers teach through both words *and* action. Therefore, their whole lives will be under the watchful eyes of all their students. The strictness that James speaks of in 3:1 is referring to a teacher's holistic integrity and righteousness.

Is there a holy union between our words and our actions, or do our actions reflect otherwise? We must be brave enough to pray on these sobering questions for our ultimate good. We can either stay in a state of contradiction or return to a state of righteousness through Christ.

Reflection

As the Holy Spirit leads us, we must repent of the contradictions between our speech and wholeness of conduct. Reflect on how your speech and actions have contradicted each other in any way during the past week.

Father God, align my words with my life. May I speak only truth and praise Your name. More of You and less of me.

Day 12

*"The tongue also is a fire, a world of evil among the parts
of the body. It corrupts the whole body, sets the whole
course of one's life on fire, and is itself set on fire by hell.
All kinds of animals, birds, reptiles and sea creatures are
being tamed and have been tamed by mankind, but no
human being can tame the tongue. It is a restless evil, full
of deadly poison. With the tongue we praise our Lord and
Father, and with it we curse human beings, who have been
made in God's likeness. Out of the same mouth come praise
and cursing. My brothers and sisters, this should not be.
Can both fresh water and salt water flow from the same
spring? My brothers and sisters, can a fig tree bear olives,
or a grapevine bear figs? Neither can a salt spring produce
fresh water."*
James 3:6-12

The metaphors James uses to decry the tongue may be
perplexing to us as modern readers, but he seems to sug-
gest that the tongue makes a life of righteousness nearly
impossible. James associates the tongue with "fire" three
times in James 3:6. It is an untamable, wild evil that is "a
restless evil, full of deadly poison." The tongue seems to
be an irredeemable evil: harmful to life and synonymous
with sin itself. However, we miss the usage and purpose
of James' metaphors when we only see the tongue as evil.

Beneath the showy, mystical analogies, the message of
3:7-8 stems from 3:6 referring to the tongue as "a world
of evil." James is not talking only about our tongues.
Rather, he is referring to the untamable nature of sin.
The sins in our lives are manifested through our tongues,
and they reflect the condition of our hearts. James focuses on living with holistic integrity before God. We
are able to know how we are walking with God when we

link our speech back to our hearts.

In 3:9-12, he reemphasizes the principle of holistic living before God in full integrity. In the same way that springs cannot produce both fresh water and salt water, James stresses that there cannot be any sort of duality between what we say and what we do. Our hearts can only be of one nature, either unrighteous or righteous, because of our faith in Jesus Christ.

Who can summarize James' point better than his blood brother, Jesus Christ? In Luke 6:45, Christ said, "A good man brings good things out of the good stored up in his heart, and an evil man brings evil things out of the evil stored up in his heart. For the mouth speaks what the heart is full of."

We must rely on the power of the Holy Spirit to convict us and act upon those convictions! There can be no duality. We are either living under the bondage of our old sinful nature or in the new covenant with Christ. James and Jesus make it clear that there is no middle ground!

Let's spend some time this morning in asking our Lord Jesus Christ to cleanse us. May we act in obedience upon the convictions the Holy Spirit places in our hearts!

Reflection
Carefully reflect on your words from yesterday.

- Did your words lift up those around you or bring them down?
- Did your words lift yourself up in pride or lift up the name of the Lord?
- Did your words share about God's love and Word with anyone around you?
- How do you want to speak today? What do you want to say and to whom?

Tame my tongue, discipline it, and teach it. Make my ears sensitive to the Holy Spirit and my heart obedient to Your convictions.

Day 13

"Who is wise and understanding among you? Let them show it by their good life, by deeds done in the humility that comes from wisdom. But if you harbor bitter envy and selfish ambition in your hearts, do not boast about it or deny the truth. Such "wisdom" does not come down from heaven but is earthly, unspiritual, demonic. For where you have envy and selfish ambition, there you find disorder and every evil practice."
James 3:13-16

In this passage, there is an alternating pattern of writing that highlights the differences between godly, meek wisdom and unspiritual, earthly wisdom. Paul speaks about these two different types of wisdom in 1 Corinthians 1:28-30:

> God chose the lowly things of this world and the despised things – and the things that are not – to nullify the things that are, so that no one may boast before him. It is because of him that you are in Christ Jesus, who has become for us wisdom from God – that is, our righteousness, holiness and redemption.

Godly wisdom has a thorough absence of all self-boasting in the presence of God. James knew that the heart could only have one nature, so he pleads with his readers, especially those who are ambitious in spirit, to not reject the wisdom that is from God. Instead, he explains that wisdom from heaven above is manifested in Christ alone and characterized by imitating His meekness (Phil. 2:3-8). Without Him, we would be utterly lost in a wisdom that is demonic and without redemption from sin.

The crux of the matter we face is this: Jesus Christ, our Lord and Savior, said in his first sermon, "Blessed are the meek, for they shall inherit the earth" (Matt. 5:5). As Christians, we know this is the third Beatitude. However, when cross-referenced with James, we see that living in a spirit of meekness would be deemed as unwise in the secular world, which would consider this godly meekness as foolish and backwards. Many contemporary Christians fall into the same category of selfish believers that James is addressing and are in danger of erroneously subscribing to a demonic wisdom that is entirely opposite of God, who is our true wisdom. Though the message that James preached is ancient, it is still relevant to us today!

The Bible does not speak about our personal preferences, conveniences, or inconveniences. It explains how to live righteously in the Lord and decries with unapologetic candor the sinful living that is in direct opposition to His living Word. We can either direct our hearts towards the words of Christ in Matthew 5:5, echoed by His brother James, or we can go along with the world.

This morning, take some time and be courageous. Wrestle with the selfish ambitions you have in your heart and repent of them.

May the Lord grant you obedience and understanding to live in a way that honors Him with the meekness of true spiritual wisdom.

Reflection

What are the selfish ambitions in your heart today? Take time to prayerfully identify them and write them down here. In your prayers, surrender them to the Lord and ask for the wisdom of heaven.

Forgive me, Lord, for the envy and self-ambition that I have harbored within. Cleanse my heart motives and draw me back into a lifestyle of humility. Make me live for the audience of One!

Day 14

"But the wisdom that comes from heaven is first of all pure;
then peace-loving, considerate, submissive, full of mercy
and good fruit, impartial and sincere. Peacemakers who
sow in peace reap a harvest of righteousness."
James 3:17-18

In James 3:13-16, James tells us that the wisdom that does not come from God is the polar opposite of meekness – i.e., entirely self-glorifying, selfishly ambitious, and an earthly wisdom that is completely devoid of God. In today's passage, James describes what the wisdom of God is like.

James emphasizes that true wisdom from God is, above all else, pure. The word "pure" used in 3:17 is ἁγνός (*hagnós*). It refers not only to the pureness of one's heart (Matt. 5:8) but also bears a connotation of sacredness, an essential quality of heavenly wisdom. This wisdom is sacred, because it comes from God himself (1 Cor. 1:30), and within Christ "are hidden all the treasures of wisdom and knowledge" (Col. 2:3). Having understood this, we see that James did not merely have godly wisdom in mind, as if laboring himself upon this would be worth his time. No, he was also leading believers to see that behind godly wisdom is the God from whom all things flow!

Thus, to have the wisdom from above means that we share in the spirit and mind of Christ (1 Cor. 2:16), and if we indeed share in the same Spirit, then, we also reap the fruit of the Spirit that are listed in Galatians 5:22-23: love, joy, peace, forbearance, kindness, goodness, faithfulness, gentleness, and self-control. Then, at long last, those who share in God's Spirit will produce a harvest of righteousness after living a life in godly wisdom.

In our previous passage, the end of James 3:16 speaks of "every evil practice" under the umbrella of the earthly, demonic wisdom. However, at the end of 3:18, James mentions a harvest of righteousness for those who sow in peace, under the umbrella of the heavenly wisdom from God. Therefore, as we study the Word, we are faced with a very natural question: Which type of wisdom are we seeking? Although we may assume this or that, the best way to answer this question is to observe the fruit that we are bearing in our lives.

At the end of the day, we are either reaping "every evil practice" or "a harvest of righteousness." James boldly declares that there is no middle ground – we are one or the other.

As you pray before the Lord, repent earnestly of all your selfish ambitions and the earthly wisdom to which you have been giving your heart. Reset and refocus your eyes upon the wisdom of the Lord. Live your life according to His Word: aligned, filled, and guided by His Spirit!

Reflection
James describes the difference between earthly wisdom and heavenly wisdom. Think about your daily actions, your work, your speech, and your interactions. How are your daily actions influenced by earthly wisdom? How do you want your daily actions to reflect God's heavenly wisdom? Be specific about which daily actions you want to take with heavenly wisdom.

Fill me up with the wisdom from above and raise me up, O Lord, to be a peacemaker in my city and in my land! I hunger to see a harvest of righteousness in this world!

Day 15

"What causes fights and quarrels among you? Don't they come from your desires that battle within you? You desire but do not have, so you kill. You covet but you cannot get what you want, so you quarrel and fight. You do not have because you do not ask God. When you ask, you do not receive, because you ask with wrong motives,that you may spend what you get on your pleasures. You adulterous people, don't you know that friendship with the world means enmity against God? Therefore, anyone who chooses to be a friend of the world becomes an enemy of God."
James 4:1-4

Today's text is applicable to any kind of quarrel, but in its time, it was most likely addressing conflicts within the church. James considers fighting in the church to be a serious sin, referring to the disputers as "adulterous people" in James 4:4. Have you ever seen this indictment applied to fighting people anywhere else? According to Merriam-Webster American Dictionary, adultery is "voluntary sexual intercourse between a married man and someone other than his wife or between a married woman and someone other than her husband." How could this relate to those who fight in the church?

Through the illumining of the Holy Spirit, James explains that people who fight, leave the church, or create cliques are motivated by their own "desires that battle within." The word "desire" in James 4:1 is ἡδονή or, when transliterated, *hēdonē*. *Hēdonē* is the Koine Greek word from which the English word "hedonism" is derived. Selfish people in the church will inevitably quarrel. We consider statements like "this church is boring" or "I am not getting anything from this cell group" as casual or even innocent, but James begs to differ. Resentment may begin small, but this is the sort of attitude that breaks churches and leads to divorces. The sentiment rings loudly as, "You don't make me 'happy' anymore, babe!" As people of God, we are in covenant relationships, and adulterous spirits break covenants.

Hedonistic "happiness"-seekers will never be satisfied. They may even "kill" (4:2) the people around them. Have you ever seen couples that suffer from infidelity? It's one of the greatest pains a human being can endure. Adulterers subject their partners to a slow, agonizing death of the spirit.

I have had youth group students who have witnessed their parents cutting ties with their churches. As a result, many of them have refused to invest in deeper relationships again. They have difficulty trusting and loving church leaders, which directly hinders their growth in Christ. Some have abandoned the church entirely as adults. Like adulterers, our selfish dissentions kill the church and its testimony. What can we do to address our thirst for selfishness?

God tells us that He will quench that inner thirst. Unlike 4:1 and 4:3, the word for "desire" in 4:2 is not *hēdonē* but ἐπιθυμεῖτε. *Epithumeite* means a mega or super desire. God has made us as finite beings, but one thing that is infinite within us is an insatiable "super desire" that cannot be satisfied by three-dimensional pleasures. It is a yearning for eternity and only our super God, the same God whom the woman at the well thirsted for in John 4:7-26.

Stop fighting over earthly love, envying worldly travel, and coveting rich foods! Kneel and seek the only One who will satisfy!

Reflection
What have you been trying to fill your super desire with?
Take your time reflecting and write your thoughts below.

*Father, forgive me for becoming friends with this world. I re-
pent for loving this world, its desires, and its things. I repent
for my worldly and materialistic dream. I repent for treat-
ing other people according to what they have and how they
look. Have mercy on me God and please make my heart
undivided and complete, sold out for You, Jesus.*

Day 16

*"Or do you think Scripture says without reason that he
jealously longs for the spirit he has caused to dwell in us?
But he gives us more grace. That is why Scripture says:
"God opposes the proud but shows favor to the humble."
Submit yourselves, then, to God. Resist the devil, and he
will flee from you. Come near to God and he will come
near to you. Wash your hands, you sinners, and purify
your hearts, you double-minded. Grieve, mourn and wail.
Change your laughter to mourning and your joy to gloom.
Humble yourselves before the Lord, and he will lift you up."*
James 4:5-10

"There's little difference in ethical behavior between the
churched and the unchurched. There's as much pilferage
and dishonesty among the churched as the unchurched.
And I'm afraid that applies pretty much across the board:
religion, per se, is not really life changing. People cite it as
important, for instance, in overcoming depression – but it
doesn't have primacy in determining behavior."

– George Gallup

When James wrote today's passage, the people he addressed were the same that George H. Gallup referred to.
Things haven't changed much from James' time to ours. Jesus even explained the nature of human behavior in Matthew 13 with His parables about the Kingdom of Heaven.
Unfortunately for the Church of Jesus Christ, weeds and
wheat will grow together until the Master will separate the
two at the end of time.

James' beseeching for true and thorough repentance
must not be taken for granted. Good trees must bear good
fruit. To gain real trust in God's provision, we must begin by turning from our wicked ways. After abandoning

our wickedness, we must be committed to remaining pure to the point of agony, as the author of Hebrews says in Hebrews 12:4, "In your struggle against sin, you have not yet resisted to the point of shedding your blood."

Because we are born into sin and raised with it, repenting completely seems nearly impossible. Many believers have given up after being blinded by years of compromise. Some look for authors and preachers that would lighten the load by compromising the Gospel with pop psychology and philosophy, but God's truths are eternal. The fact that our hearts can still be convicted is a sign of God's resilient grace!

We must repent! Imagine if my loved ones were murdered in cold blood and I ended up befriending the killer, visiting him often and even having lunch with him. Does this make any sense to anybody? What would you say? Wouldn't it perhaps seem as if I conspired with the killer to eliminate my family?

This is James' argument. You cannot befriend the world that killed your savior! Resist the Devil! Clean your hands! Grieve, mourn, and wail for your sins!

Reflection

Verse 8 says, "Come near to God and He will come near to you." Take time now to come near to God. Tune everything else out and reflect on whether you have been double-minded, befriending both the world and God. Come near to God in repentance and He will come near to you, as James has promised.

Here I am, Lord, for I am ready to wash my hands clean, surrender my heart, and bow down before You. Come near to me, for I cannot bear to live in my own pride any longer. Release Your favor over me, do not pass me by!

Day 17

"Brothers and sisters, do not slander one another. Any-
one who speaks against a brother or sister or judges them
speaks against the law and judges it. When you judge the
law, you are not keeping it, but sitting in judgment on it.
There is only one Lawgiver and Judge, the one who is able
to save and destroy. But you – who are you to judge your
neighbor?"
James 4:11-12

Let me share a wonderful story with you this morning.

There was a small fishing village on an island ignored by the rest of the world. Its inhabitants were oblivious to violence, living as one big family in harmony and peace. One gloomy and rainy morning, a group of infamous pirates discovered the village. All of its men were mercilessly killed; its women, raped and buried alive. The orphaned kids were enslaved and carried off. The kids received no education, were fed poorly, and were worked all day by these barbaric men without any hope for escape.

However, the tiny island was in the realm of a benevolent king who had heard about the raid and was in a pursuit of the pirates. After a relentless search, the king caught up with the bandits, destroyed them, and rescued the children.

In his great compassion, the king adopted all the children in his kingdom. As the king returned with the newly freed, bestial children, who looked and smelled nothing like the princes and princesses in the palace, the court whispered frantically. "Who are these kids?" "Look at how they eat!" "What is this foul smell?" However, they could not do anything beyond whispering, because the children were granted mercy and favor by the king. No matter how ugly or ignorant, how broken or feeble, they were now and forever the king's children.

Now can you imagine these kids forgetting their former predicament and fighting and hurling insults at each other? Their situations were utterly hopeless. Everything they had gained was because of their new identity. How foolish would they be if they sized each other up as if they merited the blessings they now enjoyed? James put an end to dissension in the church by exposing the foolishness of slandering and judging.

We have a new identity because of Christ our King. When we slander others, we place ourselves higher than others and become their judge. Only the king who saved us has the right to pass judgment. By becoming judges, we attempt to place ourselves above the law when in truth we were all saved equally under the same grace and all live equally under the same law. By demanding judgment, we declare ourselves greater then the Lawgiver.

Reflection

Meditate on how you may have judged your brother or sister in the past week. Why did you judge him or her? How did this influence your actions toward him or her? How did it change his or her actions toward you? Bring this to the Lord and ask for forgiveness. Pray for God's presence and mercy in your brother or sister's life.

Forgive me Lord, for I have been quick with my words and have judged Your people with the law. Fill me with Your grace, season my conversations with salt, and give me eyes to see the beauty in Your people. Show me the way of forgiveness and love for my brothers and sisters.

Day 18

*"Now listen, you who say, "Today or tomorrow we will go
to this or that city, spend a year there, carry on business
and make money." Why, you do not even know what will
happen tomorrow. What is your life? You are a mist that
appears for a little while and then vanishes. Instead, you
ought to say, "If it is the Lord's will, we will live and do this
or that." As it is, you boast in your arrogant schemes. All
such boasting is evil. If anyone, then, knows the good they
ought to do and doesn't do it, it is sin for them."*
James 4:13-17

Proverbs 16:18 warns, "Pride goes before destruction, a
haughty spirit before a fall." How often do we really heed
this advice? There have been many times when I've come
across words like this, only to say to myself, "Pride and
boasting are evil! I must be careful." Yet that would be it. It
would be difficult to pinpoint an actual event or act when
I considered myself boastful. Why? Because it goes against
our nature to see ourselves as boastful people, and it is
often the case that we don't blatantly brag about ourselves.

James, however, is so down-to-earth and ingenious in
exposing our sins. There is so much wisdom and clarity
in his writing! I learn best when the lesson is visual and
practical, and James does just these things with this lesson
on arrogance. He draws a perfect picture of an arrogant
person and exemplifies that person's words and attitude
so we may judge for ourselves; and the example is dead-
on, especially for city dwellers in the 21st century who are
dominated by schedules and busyness.

If James were alive today, he would shout, "Look at
your personal schedule, immediate plans, and big loan
purchases! Where do they reflect your dependence on
God? How do they show the fragility of our lives?"

We "say," "plan," and "purchase" as if we will live forever, as if we can actually dictate our future. James says these are the marks of a boastful person! In the middle of the text, he delivers the ageless million dollar question, "What is your life?" He is continuing the theme of heavenly wisdom from chapter three: wisdom from God is humble and dependent upon Him. It recognizes the frailty of our lives. Most importantly, it urges us to take time out and meditate on God's reality instead of filling our void with constant scheduling and busyness.

We stress about the schedules we create for ourselves and find security in our busyness, as if we are more important when we are busy. James argues otherwise. We are freed when we humble ourselves in the knowledge of the Lord. Proverbs 1:7 states, "The fear of the LORD is the beginning of knowledge, but fools despise wisdom and instruction." James says our lives are brief and short, like mists that vanish into the air, so we should trust God and know that only He sustains our lives.

This morning, meditate on the reality of our human condition. Confess your weaknesses to your Sustainer and denounce your claim of self-sufficiency!

Reflection

Write down plans you have made for the next year. The next ten years.

Now surrender these plans to the Lord and pray, "If it is the Lord's will, I will do this." "Your ways are higher than mine." Find peace in surrendering your life to God.

Forgive me, that in my busyness I have forgotten that my life is but a mist. I can't bear to live my life for anything less worthy than Your kingdom. How may I live for You, my Lord? At Your word, I will go, and I will do all that You ask of me. Please speak.

Day 19

*"Now listen, you rich people, weep and wail because of
the misery that is coming on you. Your wealth has rotted,
and moths have eaten your clothes. Your gold and silver
are corroded. Their corrosion will testify against you and
eat your flesh like fire. You have hoarded wealth in the last
days. Look! The wages you failed to pay the workers who
mowed your fields are crying out against you. The cries of
the harvesters have reached the ears of the Lord Almighty.
You have lived on earth in luxury and self-indulgence. You
have fattened yourselves in the day of slaughter. You have
condemned and murdered the innocent one, who was not
opposing you."*
James 5:1-6

I recently led a revival meeting out of state and witnessed
something that really saddened my heart. One of the vol-
unteers at the church, who came to help out with last minute preparations, was panicking because she misplaced
her new smartphone. I thought she would settle down in
time for the revival that she had helped prepare regardless of her phone's whereabouts. Sadly, she rushed home
instead, foregoing the spiritual blessings that may have
greeted her. Rich or poor, we are all affected by materialism, especially in this day and age.

In an interview with *Blender*, R&B singer Mary J. Blige
was asked how she reconciles all of her jewelry with her
Christian faith. She replied, "My God is a God who wants
me to have things. He wants me to bling! He wants me to
be the hottest thing on the block. I don't know what kind
of God the rest of y'all are serving, but the God I serve says,
'Mary, you need to be the hottest thing this year, and I'm
gonna make sure you're doing that'. My God's the bomb!"

This is an example of prosperity theology, a school

of thought that claims faith in Jesus will bring a believer material riches and good health. What blasphemy! It saddens me that sects of Christianity even debate over the validity of prosperity theology as a Biblical perspective.

Blige's quote highlights the point James makes in today's passage: Christians are just as susceptible to materialism as any other group is. We will all be guilty of some kind of materialism if we are not mindful and deliberate. In the church, we hear testimonies about overcoming family problems, being healed from terminal diseases, and conquering depression. But how often do we hear people repenting from materialism, self-centeredness, and lying?

James gives us no room for compromises in James 5:1-6. He would ask Mary J. Blige, "What will happen when all your bling is gone?" If your faith in God depends on material goods, then, your faith will disappear with your goods. If my purpose is in family, friends, wealth, or jobs, when they are gone, the conclusion is obvious. Tragic!

Hear these words again with soberness, "Your gold and silver are corroded. Their corrosion will testify against you and eat your flesh like fire. You have hoarded wealth in the last days." Gold and silver do not corrode in actuality, but what James is referring to is the temporal nature of material possessions. Gold and silver are fickle companions. They frequently change hands, and they frequently leave your hands based on circumstances.

Wealth doesn't exist to be hoarded. It must be spent in worship, given back to God and utilized to bless others. Yet the more wealth you have, the greater your struggle will be. In Matthew 19:24, Jesus said, "Again I tell you, it is easier for a camel to go through the eye of a needle than for someone who is rich to enter the kingdom of God." James warns the rich about just this – the consequences of living lives of excess – in James 5:3-6.

Remember that every possession is a gift and an

opportunity from God. Self-indulgence, inaction, and comparisons with others will not let you off the hook. Check your closet. See how it's filled with clothes you don't wear anymore, dresses and shirts you've bought but only worn once. Look at how much leftover food you throw away. Count the cost of your excesses and repent!

Reflection

What is your purpose for making money or collecting things? Write down the top five reasons for why you are making money.

Reflect on who the center of your present and future plans may be. Is it you or is it God? Offer your purposes and plans into His complete control.

My wealth is not my own, I relinquish all power it has on me. Use what I have for the end time harvest, my Lord! Take it all, everything and anything, for it was never mine to keep. Here are my hands, opened and surrendered for Your kingdom.

Day 20

"Be patient, then, brothers and sisters, until the Lord's coming. See how the farmer waits for the land to yield its valuable crop, patiently waiting for the autumn and spring rains. You too, be patient and stand firm, because the Lord's coming is near."
James 5:7-8

I appreciate this epistle for its practicality, clarity, and applicability of its lessons. In today's particular passage, James addresses the purpose behind Christian patience: that we should be patient because the Lord will return.

Friction between the poor and the rich was a major source of conflict in the early church, and it still is in our world today. Oxfam, a UK-based charity, found that the world's 100 richest people earned enough in 2012 to end global poverty four times over. The executive director of Oxfam, Jeremy Hobbs, stated, "We can no longer pretend that the creation of wealth for a few will inevitably benefit the many – too often the reverse is true." He also added, "Concentration of resources in the hands of the top one per cent depresses economic activity and makes life harder for everyone else – particularly those at the bottom of the economic ladder." We have all known these facts to be true and perhaps have even had some kind of animosity towards these "selfish" groups.

"Then" in James 5:7 is referring to the selfish and abusive rich mentioned in the paragraph above. James was asking the poor, who were under direct abuse from the rich, to be patient. As you can imagine, this must have been extremely tough for poor Christians who suffered many injustices without vindication. We all struggle with envy and jealousy towards the rich because of our sinful condition. We always mutter, "Why are rich so selfish?"

and "Why don't they ever share?" when many of us would be no different in their shoes.

We know that Christ first came to us as a savior, but His Second Coming will be as the judge of all creation. The unjust will be punished while the righteous will be comforted. Rather than being depressed, we must valiantly persist in righteousness.

However, our patience must not be passive. James says that we should wait as farmers, who actively work, plant, and maintain the lot given to them by God, while looking forward to the harvest. We ought to be the salt and light, a city upon a hill with good governance, honest charity, and sound practice. By doing so, we will eventually catch the eyes of the world and expose its inconsistencies. Light cannot be suppressed for long. It eventually shines through. The early church permeated the Roman Empire by enduring and suffering through trials, not by violence.

Know that when we practice patience, we must also actively do the Lord's work, bringing forth a harvest that will have benefits beyond imagination!

Reflection

Write down the greatest trials in your life at the moment.

How did you respond to these trials in the past week?

Take time to bring your trials to the Lord. Put your trust in God who sees your pain. He is the one who will save you and develop your character through this suffering, and, as James wrote, He is coming soon.

Lord, I surrender all my trials to You! Forgive me for trying to solve them on my own. I will wait for you. I will trust in You for You alone are worthy of my trust. Help me Lord to persist and to be steadfast!

Day 21

*"Don't grumble against one another, brothers and sisters,
or you will be judged. The Judge is standing at the door!
Brothers and sisters, as an example of patience in the face
of suffering, take the prophets who spoke in the name of
the Lord. As you know, we count as blessed those who
have persevered. You have heard of Job's perseverance and
have seen what the Lord finally brought about. The Lord
is full of compassion and mercy. Above all, my brothers
and sisters, do not swear – not by heaven or by earth or by
anything else. All you need to say is a simple "Yes" or "No."
Otherwise you will be condemned."*
James 5:9-12

In James 5:7-8, James prescribes patience as a remedy for
suffering. He explains what patience is and why believers
ought to be patient. Today, James shows us what patience
in practice looks like. What a teacher! So thorough and
practical!

When people collapse under pressure, their natural
instinct is to blame others for their difficulties. Of course,
James' audience was under more grievous circumstances
than what we experience today, but we can concur that
people today still grumble against each other when under
stress.

What are our first reactions when we lose a job or get
served papers for a divorce? We blame our parents, our
spouses, our government, and even God. Bashing others
and blaming the system seem impersonal and harmless,
but they are not any different from what James is referring
to. The attitude behind the blaming is the same.

To explain the effect that patience has on our lives,
James cites the story of Job and the lives of the prophets.
When we remain patient through suffering, it produces

perseverance, character, and ultimately hope (Rom. 5:3-4). Job endured faithfully through his suffering, and in the end he was tremendously blessed. The prophets, too, were blessed, but not often with prosperity or wealth.

God's blessings may not always include prosperity and long life, but they always shape us to be more like Him, transforming us in His righteousness. This is why James ends verse 11 with God's attributes – compassion and mercy. Patience under fire makes you more like our Savior, so be joyful today in your hardships!

Finally, James rebukes swearing. People often swear in desperation to escape suffering. In *James: The IVP New Testament Commentary Series*, George M. Stulac writes that people in desperate situations "would be tempted to strike bargains with God, swearing to do one thing or another if only God would deliver them from their persecutors. Religious people have tried this kind of bargaining all through the centuries. Animists who live in fear of their gods are driven to make such promises."

Put your hope in God and remember His promises, which sustained Job and the prophets!

Reflection
How do you handle hardships today? More specifically, in what ways is your patience similar (or different) from the illustration James has given in today's text?

I declare right now that as the sun rises every morning, Your mercies are new every day. Dear Lord, I give You my heart of long suffering. Give me a new hope, and remind me of Your promises today!

Day 22

"Is anyone among you in trouble? Let them pray. Is anyone happy? Let them sing songs of praise. Is anyone among you sick? Let them call the elders of the church to pray over them and anoint them with oil in the name of the Lord. And the prayer offered in faith will make the sick person well; the Lord will raise them up. If they have sinned, they will be forgiven."
James 5:13-15

As James nears the end of his epistle, he fittingly concludes all the discussed matters with calls for prayer. From the very beginning and throughout the letter's entirety, we sensed the great trouble with which his audience was faced. What letter begins with a greeting like this: "Consider it pure joy ... whenever you face trials" (James 1:2)?

We also know that James' audience struggled with favoritism (2), verbal abuse (3), dissension (4), and oppression from the rich (5). This community was in big trouble! In the previous passages, James calls for patience and exposes his audience of their judgments toward each other and their swearing in times of desperation. In this passage, he asks them to "put off" the old way and "put on" the new way through *prayer*.

James created a detailed list for occasions that call for prayer:

1. When we are in trouble (13a)
2. When we are successful (13b)
3. When we are sick (14-15a)
4. When we are in sin (15b-16)

Basically, we ought to pray in all circumstances, because God Himself is the answer to all of our needs and problems.

This is indicative of Paul's encouragements to the Thessalonians in 1 Thessalonians 5:16-18 when he writes, "Rejoice always, pray continually, give thanks in all circumstances; for this is God's will for you in Christ Jesus."

James shows what effective prayers look like in four essential points:

1. **Call the elders of the church.** Elders have been bestowed with power and authority (Matt. 16:18). Calling upon them is symbolic of our submission and obedience to Christ. Because there is power in numbers, the elders are promoted to organize corporate prayers, which also unite the church under authority. Just as the disciples learned how to pray from Jesus, we must learn how to pray from spiritually mature people.

2. **Anoint them with oil.** In the Bible, oil is used as a symbol of health, vitality, and the presence of God. This is why kings were anointed with oil. Through the anointing of oil, the weak in faith were reminded of God's presence and the promise of His healing. In Christ's time, it was additionally used as medicine, so it also encouraged believers to seek out conventional medical care for their ailments. In all forms of healing, we should pray and acknowledge that He is still in control.

3. **In the name of Jesus.** In Acts 4:12, Peter preached, "Salvation is found in no one else, for there is no other name under heaven given to mankind by which we must be saved." We understand the source of our power. Jesus is not a magical creature who appears when we chant repeatedly. He is our Lord and our companion. Our union with Christ and our surrender to Him are what invite His healing and presence.

Daily Devotionals

4. **Prayer in faith.** James touches upon this in James 1:5-8. A prayer of faith is lifted up with complete trust in the Lord, free from doubt and single-mindedness.

Reflection
Do you pray upon every aspect and decision in your life?
Are your prayers effective? How can you make practical
changes to your prayer life today based on what you've
read?

*Teach me to beseech You, O Lord. Not just to pray when I
am weak, but to seek Your face in all circumstances of my
life. May my prayers be aligned with Your heart in the deep-
est of intimacy, fill them with Your power and authority!*

Day 23

"Therefore confess your sins to each other and pray for each other so that you may be healed. The prayer of a righteous person is powerful and effective. Elijah was a human being, even as we are. He prayed earnestly that it would not rain, and it did not rain on the land for three and a half years. Again he prayed, and the heavens gave rain, and the earth produced its crops."
James 5:16-18

In this passage, James continues to encourage prayer and cites the life of Elijah. By characterizing the prophet as just "a human being" in James 5:17, James is inviting *all* people to pray! We do not need a special anointing to pray. All of us, regardless of status, history, or circumstance, can petition the Lord about anything. The only requirement is honesty.

However, 5:16 seems to contradict 5:17, because it adds some conditions to prayer. Praying for each other makes sense, but why must we confess our sins to one another? Was James promoting the Catholic Sacrament of Penance? Why should we confess our sins to each other if we have already confessed it to the Lord? How is it related to healing? When I became a pastor, I struggled with that verse, yet after years of ministry, I have realized why confession is a vital part of healthy spiritual living.

First, sin can have physical consequences. In Luke 5:17-26, some men brought a paralyzed man to Jesus, and He shouted, "Friend, your sins are forgiven. ... I tell you, get up, take your mat and go home." The paralyzed man immediately stood up, gathered his mat, and went home praising God. Not all sicknesses are the result of sin, but in some cases, confession and repentance are necessary for bodily healing.

Second, all of our sins are ultimately against God Himself, which is why we confess them through our mediator, Jesus Christ. If Jesus is our Ultimate Conciliator, why do we have to confess our sins to each other? It's because most of the time, we're against each other! The consequences of sin always influence people around us, especially our church community. This was the environment of James' audience.

In Matthew 5:23-24, Jesus said:

> Therefore, if you are offering your gift at the altar and there remember that your brother or sister has something against you, leave your gift there in front of the altar. First go and be reconciled to them; then come and offer your gift.

Confessing to our community brings healing to our communities. It mends broken relationships and covers over the transgressions we make against one another.

Lastly, the word "confess" in James 5:16 is transliterated as *exomologisthe* and translated from ἐξομολογέω. It means to profess and acknowledge openly, but like many Koine Greek words, it has additional connotations that cannot be simply translated as "confession." *Exomologisthe* is a public confession that is done in honor, something that is to be praised and accepted with joy, whereby the confessor also promises to act after receiving forgiveness.

Vulnerability is a prerequisite of love. C.S. Lewis articulates this claim beautifully in *The Four Loves* when he says, "To love at all is to be vulnerable. Love anything and your heart will be wrung and possibly broken. If you want to make sure of keeping it intact you must give it to no one, not even an animal. Wrap it carefully round with hobbies and little luxuries; avoid all entanglements. Lock it up safe in the casket or coffin of your selfishness. But in that casket, safe, dark, motionless, airless, it will change. It will not be broken; it will become unbreakable, impenetrable, irredeemable. To love is to be vulnerable."

Our church, Grace Community Chapel, has been a firm advocate of confession and vulnerability in our discipleship. Though it is initially painful, we have found it to be therapeutic and restorative in the long run. When a person can share honestly, it means he or she is confident in God's forgiveness and acceptance. This kind of transparency brings the church together, removes superficiality, and imparts healing that is genuine and enduring.

Reflection

Take time this morning to reflect on your sins from this week and repent before the Lord. Then, at the next cell group meeting, prayer meeting, or a meeting with a brother or sister, take time to confess your sins and ask for prayer and, if necessary, forgiveness. This is not easy to do, so take the space here to write down your confession and how you plan to share it.

Dear Lord, I confess my heart before You. Help me to open my heart, and give me the courage to confess, for I want to be healed, I want to be free. No more captives, no more prisoners in Jesus' name!

Day 24

*"My brothers and sisters, if one of you should wander from
the truth and someone should bring that person back,
remember this: Whoever turns a sinner from the error
of their way will save them from death and cover over a
multitude of sins."*
James 5:19-20

What an ending! This ending reminds me of John 4:23:

> Yet a time is coming and has now come
> when the true worshipers will worship
> the Father in the Spirit and in truth, for
> they are the kind of worshipers the Father
> seeks.

As well as the Great Commission in Matthew 28:19-20:

> Therefore go and make disciples of all na-
> tions, baptizing them in the name of the
> Father and of the Son and of the Holy
> Spirit, and teaching them to obey every-
> thing I have commanded you. And surely
> I am with you always, to the very end of
> the age.

James concludes everything by encouraging his readers to
save one another from the error of their ways, reiterating
the ultimate purpose in all of our endeavors. James' per-
vasive emphasis on righteousness was inspired by God's
holiness. In John 14:6, when Jesus said, "I am the way and
the truth and the life. No one comes to the Father except
through me," He explained that "truth" is necessary to
draw near to God. As James explains, truth practiced in

the Spirit through prayer and dependence on God glorifies Him. When we glorify Him, we draw closer to Him and to each other.

James does not mention worship at all in his letter, but the remedies, lessons, and encouragements he delivers to his audiences constitute a form of worship unto God.

The most famous question in the *Westminster Shorter Catechism* asks:

> Q. What is the chief end of man?
> A. Man's chief end is to glorify God, and
> to enjoy Him forever.

This response is an echo of what James describes throughout his epistle. We enjoy God by persistently practicing the truth through the Spirit.

In *Let the Nations Be Glad!: The Supremacy of God in Missions*, Reverend John Piper writes:

> Missions is not the ultimate goal of the church. Worship is. Missions exists because worship doesn't. Worship is ultimate, not missions, because God is ultimate, not man. When this age is over, and the countless millions of the redeemed fall on their faces before the throne of God, missions will be no more. It is a temporary necessity. But worship abides forever.

Piper's perspective on missions is consistent with James' final remarks. We have been delivered from our sins and given eternal purpose and joy! What can be more important in this life than that? In all we do, we turn back sinners and share in this forgiveness.

Jesus has called us to be fishers of men. Boats that do not fish are not fulfilling the Master's call. If you are floating without a purpose or wasting your gifts and influence on luxury instead of bringing men and women to Christ, *you are being disobedient.*

Brothers and sisters, a ship in harbor is safe, but that is not why ships are built! Raise your anchors, unfurl your sails, and strike out to find those who are wandering from the truth!

As James says, let us endure trials and temptations with joy, be quick to listen and slow to speak, throw away our prejudice, verify our faith through our deeds, bridle our tongues, hold to heavenly wisdom, submit to God, cease our boasting about tomorrow, rid ourselves of our indulgences and luxuries, be patient in our suffering, pray ceaselessly for one another in all matters, and turn sinners away from the jaws of death!

Amen!

Reflection
"Boats that do not fish are not fulfilling the Master's call."
Are you actively sharing the Gospel with the people God
placed in your life? Reflect on this question and write
down the name of just one person that you want to actively share God's love with.

It is not enough to just think and plan. How will you catch
fish by idling away in your boat? Think of one action that
you can take this week to pursue this person. It may be a
dinner, a gift, a conversation, or bringing him or her to
church. Write it down and commit it to the Lord.

During cell group (or any Christian gathering) this week,
share the name of this one person. Ask those in your cell
group to pray with you for him or her. This is difficult to
do alone. Witness the power of the church by reaching out
to your friend with the power of your cell group and other
Christians in the church.

Dear Lord, show me who to pray for, who to speak truth to, who to lift up. I want to see Your prodigals come home again. Expand my heart with your compassion for the lost, the sick, the forgotten, and the broken hearted. It's time to set sail again with courage and vigor for the one thing that matters, Your beautiful glory and Your renown.

Inductive
Bible Studies

How to
Lead a Bible Study

Leading a Bible study may seem like an intimidating task, especially if you are not a pastor, but teaching the Bible requires more than scholarship. Loving and obeying the Bible is the highest qualification. Teachers who live out the Gospel will lead their students into experiencing the power of the Word firsthand. The Bible is poetic, philosophical, and historical, but it is first and foremost a living book.

Before each lesson, meditate upon each passage throughout the week. Ask God to reveal Himself to you and work in your life. When you do so, teach in Spirit and in truth, in testimony as well as in knowledge.

At the same time, do not neglect studying the passages so that you may provide context and inspire discussion. This guide will show you how to study, examine, and teach the passages using inductive instruction.

Most teaching is done through deductive instruction. A teacher will introduce a concept, explain it, and have the students practice it. In inductive instruction, a teacher presents examples of how a concept is used and encourages the students to piece together how a concept works. Jesus did much of His preaching using inductive logic. By asking questions and telling parables, His audience learned the Gospel using their own mental faculties. In the same way, you should guide your students and dictate only when necessary so that they may arrive at the answer with you.

This guide will show you how to determine the context of a passage and the three steps of inductive instruction: observation, interpretation, and application. The objective of each lesson is to identify what God is saying and to apply the message to our lives.

Context

Think of these passages as news stories. Journalists use something called the Five Ws to cover a story. According to the Five Ws, a report cannot be considered complete without answering these five questions:

1. **Who** was it about?
2. **What** happened?
3. **When** did it take place?
4. **Where** did it take place?
5. **Why** did it happen?

And sometimes:

6. **How** did it happen?

Studying a Bible passage is the same way. You need to ask questions that will contextualize the passage to your students. (Fun fact: The Five Ws of Journalism are derived from the Three Ws, a method of Bible study popularized in the 1880s by Professor William Cleaver Wilkinson.)

Historical Context

Who wrote this passage? For whom was it intended?
What was the genre in which it was written?
When was this written?

Where was this written?
Why was it written?

Textual Context

How is the author writing? What kind of style and voice does the author use?
What was written before and after this specific passage?
What are the major themes in this chapter?

By familiarizing ourselves with the context, we understand the writer, the audience, the historical circumstances, and the purpose of the passage. This allows us to further analyze the text with greater depth and fewer assumptions.

Close Reading

There are many ways to read. You can review your textbooks for exams, sigh over love letters from your secret admirer, leaf through fashion magazines at a doctor's office, or scan an airport LED board to check if your loved one's flight has arrived.

There are many ways to read the Bible as well. You can memorize your favorite Bible verse, skim through a chapter every day, or refer to the Scripture reading during Sunday service. Bible studies are best approached by close reading.

Religious scholars have close read holy books for thousands of years. Close reading is like being a detective. You have to pick apart every minute detail of the passage – the tense of a verb that's used, whether a noun is singular or plural, any repetition of words, the phrasing of questions, or a concept that seems to be continually emphasized. Close reading in itself has multiple approaches, but I will explain one system of close reading so that we're all on the same page.

As we discussed in the introduction, you must first

and foremost come to the Word with humility and prayer. We must learn first before we teach others, and the Humble King will only accept humble students. In 2 Timothy 3:16, Paul writes, "All Scripture is God-breathed and is useful for teaching, rebuking, correcting, and training in righteousness." All your passages are God-breathed and useful for righteousness.

Before each Bible study, lead your group in prayer and worship. Even if it is just one song accompanied by a short prayer, acknowledge God as the ultimate Teacher. We learn only because God reveals, and if we want more of His revelations, we must remain humble before Him (Isa. 46:9-10; John 20:31).

The entire Bible is a love letter to humanity, so read it like one. Savor each word and verse. Instruct your group to read the passage on their own a few times. Tell them to write down their thoughts and reflections in the margins or on a separate piece of paper.

Inductive Study Method
The Inductive Study Method is broken up into three parts:

Observation

1. Underline the main verse(s) in this passage. There can be more than one main verse.
2. Circle any keywords or phrases that stick out to you.
3. Draw a rectangle around repeated words, phrases, or ideas.
4. Draw lines between any connecting words, phrases, or ideas.
5. Write questions or thoughts about the verses in the margins.

Once everyone has had time to observe the passage, you can ask members to compare their notes with each other and discuss what they've observed.

After comparing notes, ask a couple people to share their insights with the whole group. Use their reflections to transition into the next section. You might say, "That's a great point. We'll expand on that concept when we unpack that verse. Now let's ask some important questions about this passage." If someone pitches a simple question you know the answer to, answer it! If you don't know the answer, you can respond by saying, "That's a good question. Can we come back to it when we focus on that verse? For now, let's ask some important questions about the whole passage."

Interpretation

To best interpret the passage, we have to cross-reference our observations with commentaries by theologians and historical sources. This makes it easier to answer any questions about ancient Hebrew, Koine Greek, and the context in which the passages were written. We recommend using the ESV Study Bible and *The Letter of James: An Introduction and Commentary* by Douglas J. Moo as references.

Application

After close reading and contextualizing the passage, we have a better grasp of what God is telling us. Now we must apply the text to our own lives to bolster our spiritual walk. Ask these two questions:

1. How did this passage apply to its original audience?
2. How is God speaking to me through this passage today?

You may craft more specific questions to fit the topic of the passage and the context of your members. For example, college cell group leaders teaching a Bible passage about loving your neighbors may ask, "How can I actively love a neighbor on my campus this week?"

Encourage your members to share their applications and resolutions with the rest of the group. Tell them to lift up one another in prayer so that they may obey these lessons.

Finally, organize weekly accountability through fellowship, emails, texts, and phone calls to ensure that your group is actively living out the Word.

In summary, we share applications by:

1. Sharing with the group verbally.
2. Praying for each other's convictions.
3. Keeping accountable through the week by meeting, emailing, and calling.

Closing

Acknowledge that everything we learn from the Bible is inspired and breathed out by God (2 Tim. 3:16). Begin and conclude each lesson with worship and prayer. In your closing prayer, give thanks to God for speaking to your group.

Inductive Study 1
James 1:19-27

Introduction for Leaders

The first lesson focuses on the main idea that *Christians need to act out the Word of God*. It is not enough to merely listen and understand the Bible. This lesson is a wonderful way to begin a Bible study, because the goal of our study is not to become more intelligent. Rather, the goal of our Bible study is to love God more and to obey His Word with our lives. This is exactly what James 1:19-27 is about.

As Jesus' brother, James was so intimate with the teachings of Jesus that his letter echoes Jesus' words from beginning to end. For example, James 1:2 – "Consider it pure joy, my brothers and sisters, whenever you face trials of many kinds" – echoes Jesus' sermon on the mount where Jesus told suffering believers to "Rejoice and be glad, for your reward is great in heaven" (Matt. 5:12). When Jesus warned followers of false prophets, He advised them to check their fruits, their actions: "You will recognize them by their fruits. Are grapes gathered from thornbushes, or figs from thistles? (Matt. 7:16). James echoes his brother, Jesus, again in James 3:12, "My brothers and sisters, can a fig tree bear olives, or a grapevine bear figs?"

As his letter reveals, James had experienced the salvation and power of Jesus' teachings up close and firsthand, but after the resurrection, he began to see people taking Jesus' teachings lightly. He saw believers listen and nod their heads in understanding during sermons but live the rest of their days according to their old ways, fighting, cursing, loving the world, and seeking material pleasures.

James 1:19-27 is James' rebuke to them, his primary audience, but also to us for not living out the Word of God. As you teach this passage, make sure that your group members come away with the one main idea that we must act out the Word of God. Why? James gives us his reason in 1:21. The Word has been "planted in you, which can save you." James uses the Greek word, *emphytos*, which was also the word used to describe how seeds are planted in the ground. God planted the saving gospel truth in our hearts without any help from us. This gospel truth, that Jesus' death and resurrection saved us eternally from our death in sin, has given us new life! We cannot ignore this saving Word that God has planted in our hearts, because it has given us new life, new identity, new purpose, and new hope.

Warm-up Activity

1.   What was the most important email or letter that you have received? It could have been a love letter, an acceptance letter into college, an email that you got the job, a letter from a long-lost family member, etc.

2.   Who wrote it?

3.   Why was it important?

4.   Do you remember any words, phrases, or sentences from the letter? Write it down.

5.   How did the letter change your life after reading it?

Share your responses with your group.

This Bible study will examine how great an importance the Bible has on our lives. Through this study, we will ask how much the Bible changes our daily lives.

We will begin the study by first close reading the passage. Then we will consider the context, interpret the passage, and conclude by applying it to our lives.

Observation

1. Underline the main verse(s) in this passage. Even if you're unsure, underline what you think might be the main thrust of this passage. There can be more than one.
2. Circle any key words or phrases that stick out to you.
3. Draw a rectangle around repeated words, phrases, or ideas.
4. Draw lines between any connecting words, or phrases, or ideas.
5. Write questions or notes about verses in the margin.

James 1:19-27

My dear brothers and sisters, take note of this: Everyone should be quick to listen, slow to speak and slow to become angry, [20] because human anger does not produce the righteousness that God desires. [21] Therefore, get rid of all moral filth and the evil that is so prevalent and humbly accept the word planted in you, which can save you.

²² Do not merely listen to the word, and so deceive yourselves. Do what it says.

²³ Anyone who listens to the word but does not do what it says is like someone who looks at his face in a mirror ²⁴ and, after looking at himself, goes away and immediately forgets what he looks like. ²⁵ But whoever looks intently into the perfect law that gives freedom, and continues in it – not forgetting what they have heard, but doing it – they will be blessed in what they do.

Context

1. Based on this passage and the rest of James, what do you think the audience was like?

2. If James were reading this out loud, what kind of tone do you think he would use when reading it?

3. What other contextual factors (location, author, audience, time, reason for writing) can you gather from reading this?

Interpretation

Read through the verses with your group. Try to identify the main idea of the passage and see how James develops the idea through the use of key words, analogies, and exhortations. See how James defines the Word of God. Use this space to record insights.

Application

1. How did this passage apply to the readers back then?

2. How does God speak to me through this passage today?

3. (Cell-group specific question)

Sharing Applications

1. Share with your group verbally.
2. Pray for one another's resolutions and convictions.
3. Keep accountable through the week by meeting, emailing, or calling.

Closing

End with a time of worship and prayer.

Inductive Study 2
James 2:14-26

Introduction for Leaders

The second study teaches the main idea that *our faith needs to be active and alive*. We focus on a passage that has been fiercely debated by theologians for centuries. James 2:14-26 has been a difficult passage to study for its focus on the law, but once we look more carefully at how James understood the law, we will see why this passage is so important for our faith.

To begin, James is not preaching that we are saved by our actions. From our first study, we remember that James preached that it is through the Word that we are saved (1:21), and this is not our doing but rather completely God's. He planted His truth of the gospel in our hearts through the Holy Spirit. Then what does James mean when he says in 2:24, "You see that a person is considered righteous by what they do and not by faith alone"? Doesn't this contradict what Paul says in Romans 3:28, "For we maintain that a person is justified by faith apart from the works of the law"? What does James mean here?

First, when James says that someone is not "considered righteous ... by faith alone," he is talking about a dead faith that does not truly have a genuine relationship and personal trust in Jesus Christ. James is saying that it is not enough just to hear the gospel or to understand it. One must hear it and enact it in order to truly have faith. Therefore, the verse can be read as saying that we cannot be considered righteous by dead faith alone. Rather, our faith needs to bear fruit in action and in our deeds.

Furthermore, James says that Abraham was "considered righteous" for his works (2:21). James is not arguing that Abraham's works is what gave him salvation. Rather, he is asserting that Abraham's works demonstrated that Abraham had been already saved, as evidenced by the good works that he did. In other words, Abraham's good works were evidence that he had salvation. The Greek word used here, *dikaioō*, emphasizes the idea that works demonstrate that someone has already been justified. Thus, James praises Abraham for having a living and active faith that leads to good works. The importance of active faith bearing fruit is also seen in the teachings of Jesus (Matt. 7:15-20) and later in Paul (Gal. 5:22-23).

Notice finally that the good works James preaches is not the legalistic kind of obedience that Pharisees had taught. James does not discuss what one eats, wears, or ritually practices as in the Jewish law. Rather he focuses on the acts of love to others (James 2:14-19) that Jesus had emphasized to His followers in His teachings (John 15:9-17). Our acts of love are possible, because God first loved us (1 John 4:19).

Warm-up Activity

1. Identify one person in your life who claims that he or she loves you. Write his or her name down.

2. What are three tangible things he or she has done to prove their love to you in the past month?

3. Imagine that this person stopped showing his or her love to you but claimed that he or she still loved you (only through words). How would you respond to him or her?

This Bible study will examine the difference between true love and false love, true faith and false faith.

We will begin the study by first close reading the passage. Then we will consider the context, interpret the passage, and conclude by applying it to our lives.

Observation

1. Underline the main verse(s) in this passage. Even if you're unsure, underline what you think might be the main thrust of this passage. There can be more than one.
2. Circle any key words or phrases that stick out to you.
3. Draw a rectangle around repeated words, phrases, or ideas.
4. Draw lines between any connecting words, or phrases, or ideas.
5. Write questions or notes about verses in the margin.

James 2:14-26

What good is it, my brothers and sisters, if someone claims to have faith but has no deeds? Can such faith save them? [15] Suppose a brother or a sister is without clothes and daily food. [16] If one of you says to them, "Go in peace; keep warm and well fed," but does nothing about their physical needs, what good is it? [17] In the same way, faith by itself, if it is not accompanied by action, is dead.

¹⁸ But someone will say, "You have faith; I have deeds." Show me your faith without deeds, and I will show you my faith by my deeds. ¹⁹ You believe that there is one God. Good! Even the demons believe that—and shudder. ²⁰ You foolish person, do you want evidence that faith without deeds is useless? ²¹ Was not our father Abraham considered righteous for what he did when he offered his son Isaac on the altar? ²² You see that his faith and his actions were working together, and his faith was made complete by what he did. ²³ And the scripture was fulfilled that says, "Abraham believed God, and it was credited to him as righteousness," and he was called God's friend. ²⁴ You see that a person is considered righteous by what they do and not by faith alone. ²⁵ In the same way, was not even Rahab the prostitute considered righteous for what she did when she gave lodging to the spies and sent them off in a different direction? ²⁶ As the body without the spirit is dead, so faith without deeds is dead.

Context

1. Based on this passage and the rest of James, what problems might the audience be dealing with?

2. If James were reading this out loud, what kind of tone do you think he would use when reading it? How do you think James felt as he wrote this?

3. What other contextual factors (location, author, audience, time, reason for writing) can you gather from reading this?

Interpretation

Read through the verses with your group. Try to identify the main idea of the passage and see how James develops the idea through the use of key words, analogies, and exhortations. See how James defines faith. Use this space to record insights.

Application

1. How did this passage apply to the readers back then?

2. How does God speak to me through this passage today?

3. (Cell-group specific question)

Sharing Applications

1. Share with your group verbally.
2. Pray for one another's resolutions and convictions.
3. Keep accountable through the week by meeting, emailing, or calling.

Closing
End with a time of worship and prayer.

Inductive Study 3
James 3:13-4:4

Introduction for Leaders

The third study will teach the main idea that *Biblical wisdom is enacting God's love*. There are many different ideas of wisdom. Some may argue that a wise person intellectually knows everything about their specialization. Some may argue that a wise person has endured all types of life experiences. Some may claim that a wise person has perception into the future. In today's passage, James teaches us a Biblical wisdom that radically departs from any earthly sort of wisdom.

James describes wisdom from heaven as "pure" (James 3:17). In Greek, the word *hagnos* is used, which means innocent and blameless. According to James, wisdom is pure from envy, selfish ambition, and malice towards others. In other words, wisdom is like selflessness. Put another way, wisdom is God-fulness. When we are full of God's spirit, then, we may grow in this wisdom that causes us to submit to others, create peace, and give freely.

This definition of wisdom is very different from other conceptions of wisdom that focus on a selfish idea of what one knows or possesses to demonstrate his or her wisdom. James teaches us that God's Biblical wisdom is the wisdom of the meek and humble (3:13) who submits first to God and then to others, not out of weakness but out of trust in God.

James' idea of wisdom is a very practical one. As Christians, we can practice and grow in this wisdom through actively serving those around us. This Bible study will not only teach a new notion of wisdom but encourage your group to practice this heavenly wisdom today.

Warm-up Activity

What are some words that come to mind when you think of secular wisdom? Write those words down in the top circle. Write words down for Biblical wisdom in the bottom circle. Write any words that count for both secular wisdom and Biblical wisdom in the middle.

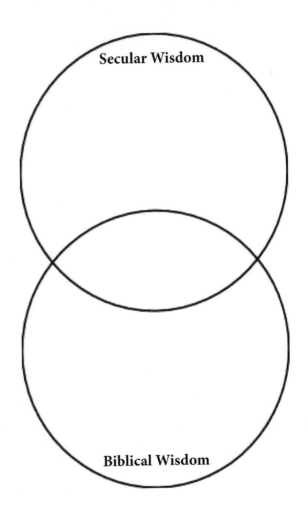

This Bible study will examine the way God defines wisdom.

We will begin the study by first close reading the passage. Then we will consider the context, interpret the passage, and conclude by applying it to our lives.

Observation

1. Underline the main verse(s) in this passage. Even if you're unsure, underline what you think might be the main thrust of this passage. There can be more than one.
2. Circle any key words or phrases that stick out to you.
3. Draw a rectangle around repeated words, phrases, or ideas.
4. Draw lines between any connecting words, or phrases, or ideas.
5. Write questions or notes about verses in the margin.

James 3:13-4:4

Who is wise and understanding among you? Let them show it by their good life, by deeds done in the humility that comes from wisdom. [14] But if you harbor bitter envy and selfish ambition in your hearts, do not boast about it or deny the truth. [15] Such "wisdom" does not come down from heaven but is earthly, unspiritual, demonic. [16] For where you have envy and selfish ambition, there you find disorder and every evil practice. [17] But the wisdom that comes from heaven is first of all pure; then peace-loving, considerate, submissive, full of mercy and good fruit, impartial and sincere. [18] Peacemakers who sow in peace reap a harvest of righteousness.

4 [1] What causes fights and quarrels among you? Don't they come from your desires that battlewithin you? [2] You desire but do not have, so you kill. You covet but you cannot get what you want, so you quarrel and fight. You do not have because you do not ask God. [3] When you ask, you do not receive, because you ask with wrong motives, that you may spend what you get on your pleasures. [4] You adulterous people, don't you know that friendship with the world means enmity against God? Therefore, anyone who chooses to be a friend of the world becomes an enemy of God.

Context

1. Based on this passage and the rest of James, what problems might the audience be dealing with?

2. If James were reading this out loud, what kind of tone do you think he would use when reading it? How do you think James felt as he wrote this?

3. What other contextual factors (location, author, audience, time, reason for writing) can you gather from reading this?

Interpretation

Read through the verses with your group. Try to identify the main idea of the passage and see how James develops the idea through the use of key words, analogies, and exhortations. See how James defines wisdom. Use this space to record insights.

Application

1. How did this passage apply to the readers back then?

2. How does God speak to me through this passage today?

3. (Cell-group specific question)

Sharing Applications

1. Share with your group verbally.
2. Pray for one another's resolutions and convictions.
3. Keep accountable through the week by meeting, emailing, or calling.

Closing
End with a time of worship and prayer.

Inductive Study 4
James 5:7-12

Introduction for Leaders

The final study will focus on the main idea that *Jesus will surely come again soon!* The book of James begins and ends with the same advice to believers. In the beginning, James urged believers to consider their sufferings pure joy (James 1:2). Here, James urges believers to be patient and firm in their sufferings. The Christians of this time suffered for reasons of persecution, poverty (as evident in the context of James), and the natural sicknesses of this world. We experience the same kinds of trials, but how are we responding to them?

This study will raise the question of how we respond to suffering in our lives. For James, there was only one reason for why it made sense to stand firm, be patient, and look at suffering as pure joy. The one reason was that Jesus, the messiah and healer of all our suffering, would be returning very, very soon. Since Jesus' Second Coming was so soon, James found his present sufferings tolerable and even enjoyable as a test of perseverance (1:2).

How do we respond to the good news that Jesus is coming? Is it something we just hear and forget? Do we truly believe that Jesus is coming? If we did, how would our lives be different? How would we respond to suffering?

Jesus commands us to be the light and salt of the world (Matt. 5:13). When the world sees how we respond to suffering, are they attracted to Christ? Or do we respond by cursing at people, complaining, making plans of revenge or escape, or numbing ourselves with entertainment and addictions? If we truly responded to suffering with pure joy and suffered with patience, wisdom, joy, endurance, perseverance, and full trust in the Lord, how brightly we would shine in this world! May this study not only redefine our suffering but also cause us to trust more fully in the Lord's promise that He is surely coming again.

Warm-up Activity

1. What was the most important promise that someone has made to you in your life?

2. Did this person keep the promise or not? How?

You may share with your group if you would like.

This Bible study will examine a promise Jesus made to us before leaving the world. We will see how this promise should change our lives and the way we see suffering.

We will begin the study by first close reading the passage. Then we will consider the context, interpret the passage, and conclude by applying it to our lives.

Observation

1. Underline the main verse(s) in this passage. Even if you're unsure, underline what you think might be the main thrust of this passage. There can be more than one.
2. Circle any key words or phrases that stick out to you.

3. Draw a rectangle around repeated words, phrases, or ideas.
4. Draw lines between any connecting words, or phrases, or ideas.
5. Write questions or notes about verses in the margin.

James 5:7-12

Be patient, then, brothers and sisters, until the Lord's coming. See how the farmer waits for the land to yield its valuable crop, patiently waiting for the autumn and spring rains. [8] You too, be patient and stand firm, because the Lord's coming is near. [9] Don't grumble against one another, brothers and sisters, or you will be judged. The Judge is standing at the door! [10] Brothers and sisters, as an example of patience in the face of suffering, take the prophets who spoke in the name of the Lord. [11] As you know, we count as blessed those who have persevered. You have heard of Job's perseverance and have seen what the Lord finally brought about. The Lord is full of compassion and mercy. [12] Above all, my brothers and sisters, do not swear – not by heaven or by earth or by anything else. All you need to say is a simple "Yes" or "No." Otherwise you will be condemned.

James

Context

1. Based on this passage and the rest of James, what problems might the audience be dealing with?

2. If James were reading this out loud, what kind of tone do you think he would use when reading it? How do you think James felt as he wrote this?

3. What other contextual factors (location, author, audience, time, reason for writing) can you gather from reading this?

Interpretation

Read through the verses with your group. Try to identify the main idea of the passage and see how James develops the idea through the use of key words, analogies, and exhortations. See how James defines our suffering and the coming of Christ. Use this space to record insights.

Application

1. How did this passage apply to the readers back then?

2. How does God speak to me through this passage today?

3. (Cell-group specific question)

Sharing Applications

1. Share with your group verbally.
2. Pray for one another's resolutions and convictions.
3. Keep accountable through the week by meeting, emailing, or calling.

Closing
End with a time of worship and prayer.

Sermons

Notes

James

Notes

Notes

Notes

Notes

Notes

Notes

Notes

Notes

Notes

5507353R00080

Made in the USA
San Bernardino, CA
09 November 2013